Fascinating Mummies

Highlights of the Exhibition

Fascinating Mummies

National Museum of Scotland
Chambers Street
Edinburgh EH1 1JF

11 February to 27 May 2012

This exhibition was developed by

National Museums Scotland
Chambers Street
Edinburgh EH1 1JF

in co-operation with

National Museum of Antiquities
(Rijksmuseum van Oudheden)
Leiden, The Netherlands

Musée de la civilisation
Québec City, Canada

www.nms.ac.uk/mummies

First published in 2012 by
NMS Enterprises Limited – Publishing
a division of NMS Enterprises Limited
National Museums Scotland
Chambers Street, Edinburgh EH1 1JF

www.nms.ac.uk

British Library Cataloguing in Publication Data
A catalogue record for this book
is available from the British Library.

ISBN: 978 1 905267 71 2

Cover design: Mark Blackadder
Cover image and title page: Coffin of Amenhotep
   (see pages 28–29). From Thebes; dated to the
   Third Intermediate Period, 21st Dynasty (*c.*1000
   BC). Image: Rijksmuseum van Oudheden (Leiden,
   The Netherlands).
Publication format:
   NMS Enterprises Limited – Publishing
Printed and bound in the United Kingdom by
   ARC Printing Ltd, West Calder

Published by National Museums Scotland as one of a
number of titles based on museum scholarship and
partnership.

For a full listing of NMS Enterprises Limited – Publishing
titles and related merchandise:

www.nms.ac.uk/books

Contents

Foreword

DR GORDON RINTOUL

DIRECTOR
NATIONAL MUSEUMS SCOTLAND

We are delighted that the first major special exhibition at the redeveloped National Museum of Scotland should be *Fascinating Mummies* in collaboration with the National Museum of Antiquities, Leiden.

The exhibition, with its lavish displays of Egyptian material, takes full advantage of our major new gallery, created as the result of the reinvention of our Victorian museum in the transformative project completed in 2011. The display of the exhibition in Edinburgh is the only United Kingdom venue of an international tour.

Material from the rich Egyptology collection of National Museums Scotland has been incorporated for the display in Edinburgh. Our collection owes much to the pioneering Scottish scholar Alexander Henry Rhind (1833–1863). His ill-health drove him to travel to Egypt where he worked on excavations at Thebes and Giza, and introduced methodical techniques to record and study the results. One of his finds, the 'Rhind' mummy and coffin, shown together with the results of recent research using modern scanning techniques, is a superb example of the insights into ancient culture offered by this exhibition.

It has been a pleasure to work with our colleagues from the National Museum of Antiquities and we thank them for making it possible to bring *Fascinating Mummies* to Scotland.

Preface

WIM WEIJLAND

DIRECTOR

NATIONAL MUSEUM OF ANTIQUITIES
LEIDEN, THE NETHERLANDS

The story of Egypt goes back thousands of years. The story of this exhibition is of a more recent date and started with the acquisition in 1828 of a large collection of Egyptian antiquities by the National Museum of Antiquities in Leiden, The Netherlands, which forms the core of the museum today.

The Egyptian collection of the National Museum of Antiquities is not only special because of its quality, or the glimpse it gives of ancient Egyptian life, but also because it binds museums and scientists worldwide. Our museum's excavations in Saqqara (Egypt), and a coffin restoration project in collaboration with the Vatican Museums, are but two examples of this.

The latest example is, of course, the collaboration with National Museums Scotland on the exhibition *Fascinating Mummies*, which has been a great experience.

I would like to thank my colleagues at National Museums Scotland for making this wonderful exhibition possible.

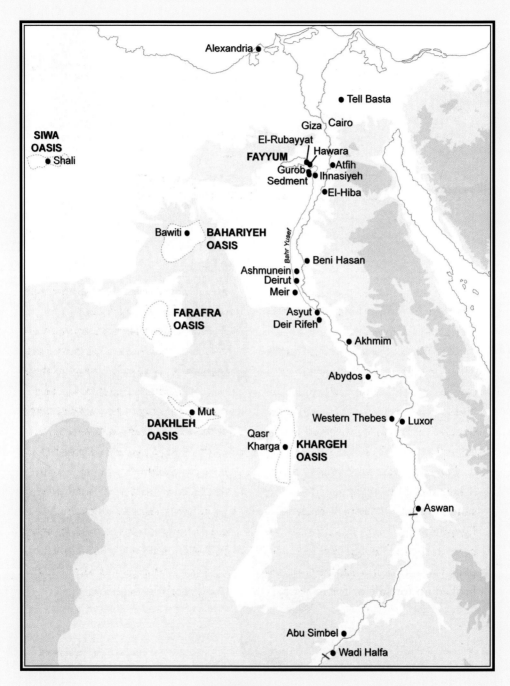

Land of the Nile

The history of ancient Egypt spans over 5000 years. This map shows some of the key sites and cities associated with the exhibits featured in this book.

LIFE EVERLASTING

For the inhabitants of ancient Egypt, dying was considered to be merely a transition into a new period of their lives, moving from this world into another. To achieve everlasting life, in both the physical and spiritual sense, the body of the deceased should be preserved and protected.

Believing that their final resting places should have provided a sanctuary for all eternity, ancient Egyptians could not have foreseen how, in the future, many burial places would be looted, the contents broken up for sale or for recycling, and the mummies themselves often mutilated or destroyed.

Mummies that have survived are valuable witnesses to the past, and they are now slowly giving up their secrets. In more recent times, new scientific technologies have allowed archaeologists and scientists to examine bodies without unwrapping them, an invasive and highly destructive process. Non-invasive techniques, such as x-rays and computerised tomography scanning (CT scanning), enable mummies to be examined in greater detail without disturbing the bodies.

Above: Limestone stela of Sehetepibreankh

The centre of this stela depicts a standard with two raised arms enclosing the name of the deceased. These two raised arms mean *ka*, the protective spirit of a person, and at the same time their vitality, identity and energy.

Abydos; Middle Kingdom,
early 12th Dynasty (*c*.1940–1900 BC)

Rijksmuseum van Oudheden
(Leiden, The Netherlands)

Opposite: *Ba* bird

This painted wooden *Ba* bird is decorated with gilding.

Late Period (*c*.715–332 BC)

Rijksmuseum van Oudheden
(Leiden, The Netherlands)

THE ETERNAL BODY

To the ancient Egyptian each person was unique, composed of an earthly body and a number of spiritual aspects, including the *ka* (life force) and the *ba* (soul). For the deceased to attain eternal life, the *ka* and *ba* had to be able to return to the earthly body, preserved and protected through mummification.

Representations of the *ba* bird flying around the deceased began to appear in tomb paintings, and in the Book of the Dead, during the New Kingdom period (1550–1070 BC).

The *ba*, a bird with a human head, left the body at death to fly freely. It travelled between the afterlife and the tomb where the mummi-fied body was laid to rest. The *ba* had to reunite regularly with the body in order to become the *akh*. As the 'effective spirit', the *akh* could even influence affairs back in the land of the living.

The *ka* was the vital life force, one of the fundamental elements in every human. After death, it had to ensure the survival of the deceased. It was the form of the spirit which acted as the channel for food and drink between the world of the living and the world of the dead.

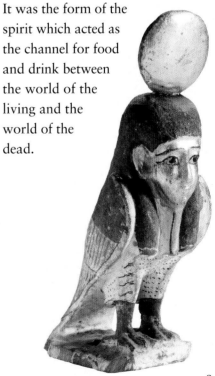

Timeline

THE DYNASTIES OF ANCIENT EGYPT

PREDYNASTIC PERIOD

4500–3000 BC

- Development of agriculture in Egypt
- Maadi and Fayyum cultures in northern Egypt
- Naqada prehistoric cultures in southern Egypt
- Naturally-mummified bodies in graves in desert
- Building of first temples at Heirakonpolis
- Development of the concept of kingship

EARLY DYNASTIC PERIOD

1st–2nd Dynasties

3000–2650 BC

- First appearance of hieroglyphs
- Unification of Upper and Lower Egypt under Narmer, the first pharaoh (*c.*3000 BC)
- Memphis is national capital
- Royal tombs at Abydos and Saqqara
- First artificial mummification
- Civil war during late 2nd Dynasty (*c.*2650 BC)

OLD KINGDOM

3rd–8th Dynasties

2650–2150 BC

- Maturity of Egyptian concept of the state
- Building of Step Pyramid, the first of all pyramids (*c.*2650 BC)
- Building of Giza pyramids by Khufu, Khaefre and Menkaure (*c.*2550–2450 BC)
- Carving of Great Sphinx at Giza (*c.*2500 BC)
- Building of sun-temples at Abusir and Abu Ghurob (*c.*2450–2375 BC)
- Longest reign in history: 94 years of Pepy II (*c.*2290–2190 BC)

FIRST INTERMEDIATE PERIOD

2150–2060 BC

- Break-up of Egypt into separate states
- Civil war leading to reunification led by kings of Thebes

MIDDLE KINGDOM

11th–13th Dynasties

2060–1650 BC

- Thebes first becomes prominent as a political and religious centre (c.2040 BC)
- Amenemhat I is assassinated (c.1965 BC)
- First temples built at Karnak, the cult-centre of the god Amun (c.1950 BC)
- Expansion of Egyptian power into Nubia (c.1950–1840 BC)
- Building of giant temple known as the 'Labyrinth' at Hawara (c.1800 BC)
- Gradual decline of central power and settlement of Palestinians in the north-east (c.1750–1650 BC)

SECOND INTERMEDIATE PERIOD

1650–1550 BC

- North of Egypt taken over by rulers from Palestine (the 'Hyksos')
- Invasion of south of Egypt by Nubians
- War of liberation by kings of Thebes

Above:

Funerary papyrus of Montsaf (detail) (also pp. 12 and 13)

Roman Period (c.9 BC)

National Museums Scotland

11

NEW KINGDOM
1550–1070 BC
18th–20th Dynasties

- Egyptian empire created in Syria-Palestine and Nubia by Thutmose I and III (c.1500–1424 BC)
- Female pharaoh Hatshepsut rules alongside Thutmose III (c.1472–1457 BC)
- Massive expansion of Karnak temples
- Akhenaten and his wife Nefertiti create the controversial cult of sole-god Aten (c.1352–1335 BC)
- Tutankhamun restores traditional religion (c.1330 BC)
- Rameses II fights battle of Qadesh against the Hittites (c.1274 BC), builds the temples at Abu Simbel (c.1250 BC), and extends the temple of Luxor

THIRD INTERMEDIATE PERIOD
21st–25th Dynasties
1070–633 BC

- Economic decline
- Reburial of robbed royal mummies in communal tombs (c.1070–920 BC)
- Rise and rule of pharaohs of Libyan origin (c.980–725 BC)
- Break-up of Egypt into separate kingdoms (c.835–725 BC)
- Reunification by kings from Nubia (c.725 BC)
- Revival of pyramid building by kings in Nubia

LATE PERIOD
26th–31st Dynasties
663–332 BC

- Reorganisation by kings from city of Sais after Assyrian invasion (663–650 BC)
- Egyptian invasion of Nubia by Psamtik II (595–589 BC)
- Persian domination (525–334 BC)
- Egyptian revival and extensive temple-building (400–342 BC)
- Re-conquest by Persia (342–332 BC)
- Conquest of Egypt by Alexander the Great (332 BC)

HELLENISTIC/ PTOLEMAIC PERIOD
1st–2nd Dynasties
332–30 BC

- Rule by Alexander the Great and his successors
- Foundation of Alexandria as new capital
- Early kings named Ptolemy expand Egyptian power around eastern Mediterranean
- Power struggles within royal family undermine Egyptian power and independence
- Extensive building and rebuilding of temples, including Philae and Dendara
- The museum and library in Alexandria become seats of learning and research
- Cleopatra VII and Mark Antony defeated by Roman Emperor Octavian (30 BC)

ROMAN PERIOD
30 BC – AD 395

- Egypt is incorporated into the Roman Empire
- Continued building and rebuilding of traditional temples, including that of Tafeh

13

PREDYNASTIC PERIOD
POTTERY PRODUCTION

(4500–3000 BC)

Agriculture first came to the Nile valley around 5000 BC, and with it came the earliest production of pottery in the area.

The types of pottery varied up and down the Nile, but the best known were those found in southern Egypt. These pottery types were named after the sites where they were first found – the Badarian and Naqada I–III.

Over the period, distinct settlements began to join together into regional political groupings that would bring together Egypt as a unified country around 3000 BC.

Most of the material associated with this period has been discovered in cemeteries, which at that time were shallow pits in the desert. The body of the deceased would have been placed into the pit in a crouched position, lying on its left side.

Pottery jar

This decorated jar has two lugs.

Abydos; Predynastic Period (c.3400 BC)

National Museums Scotland

Pottery bowl

A black-topped ware bowl typical of the earlier part of the Predynastic period.

Predynastic Period (c.3700 BC)

National Museums Scotland

Strings of beads

These beads have been made from semi-precious stones such as carnelian and lapis lazuli.

Predynastic Period (c.4000–3000 BC)

National Museums Scotland

OLD KINGDOM
THE PYRAMIDS

3RD–8TH DYNASTIES (2650–2150 BC)

The evolution of the pyramid reached its structural peak during the first half of the 4th Dynasty, during the period of the Old Kingdom. At that time, the largest of all the pyramids were built by three generations of pharaohs.

Below: Wooden model sledge

This sledge formed part of a foundation deposit at the temple of Hatshepsut and is inscribed with a text including the female king's throne name.

Deir el-Bahri; New Kingdom,
18th Dynasty (*c.*1460 BC)
National Museums Scotland

Right: Wooden butterfly cramp

Used to join together two blocks of masonry in the process of construction.

Late Period (*c.*747–332 BC)
National Museums Scotland

However, the biggest of all the pyramids belonged to the pharaoh, Khufu, and it is known today as the Great Pyramid of Giza.

The Great Pyramid contained a highly unusual layout of interior passages, thought to have been the result of changes to the plan during construction. This layout, combined with the pyramid's vast size, has prompted various theories over the years about the purpose and origins of the structure. However, there is no doubt among archaeologists that it was nothing more than a tomb built for the pharaoh, Khufu.

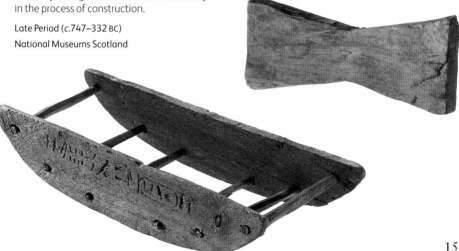

MIDDLE KINGDOM
KHNUMHOTEP
PURE PRIEST, SON OF HENIB

MID-12TH DYNASTY (c.1900–1850 BC)

Ancient Egyptian coffins from about 3000 BC until the 4th century AD generally take one of two basic shapes – rectangular and anthropoid (human-shaped).

A rectangular coffin was designed to hold a contracted body. Hieroglyphic texts were added, requesting offerings for the spirit of the deceased. A pair of *wedjat*-eyes (see detail on the opposite page), on the left side of the coffin, would allow the corpse, laid on its own left (or, in Egyptian terms, 'eastern') side, to gaze at the sunrise, or in full view of offerings for the consumption of the deceased. *Wedjat*-eyes take the form of human eyes combined with the external markings of a falcon's eyes

They are a symbol of well-being (*wadj*) and eternity.

The coffin of Khnumhotep, son of Henib, is made of wood, and is among the earliest known coffins of the period and typical of its time, with the *wedjat*-eyes decoration and hieroglyphic texts invoking offerings for his spirit.

The coffin was discovered by the Egyptian archaeologist Ahmed Kamal (1851–1923) in 1914 at Meir, Middle Egypt, in the cemetery of the governors of the district of Cusae (modern El-Quseir). The exact location of the tomb, however, is no longer known.

The coffin was owned by a man called Khnumhotep, whose mother is named as Henib. His title (*waab*, 'pure')

meant 'priest' in the language of his contemporaries.

A single column of text with a brief prayer runs down the centre of the lid, identifying the deceased and his mother. A band of text decorates the upper margins on the long sides of the trough, each giving a standard offering formula in favour of the deceased: the left side in the name of Osiris, the right side in the name of the god Anubis. The long sides each have four columns of text that tell us that Khnumhotep is revered before the gods Imseti, Shu, Tefnet and Duamutef (left side, from head to foot), and the gods Hapy, Geb, Nut and Qebehsenuef (right side, from head to foot). The head-end has a line of text invoking Nephthys and two columns naming the Great Ennead (left) and Selqet (right). The foot-end likewise has a line of text invoking Isis, and two columns invoking the Small Ennead (left) and Neith (right).

At the head on the left side of the trough, the *wedjat*-eyes are located within a black-outlined rectangle (see below). The mummy would originally have been laid on its side so that the

face of the deceased was behind this panel; and a brief inscription beneath it requests bread and beer for the spirit of the deceased.

Coffin of Khnumhotep

Khnumhotep's coffin is typical of its period, with a pair of *wedjat*-eyes (see detail below) which allowed the mummy – placed lying on its left-hand side – to see out, gazing towards the east, the land of the living. The texts on the coffin are magic formulae, conjuring up food, drink and clothing, and enveloping the coffin in the protection of gods and goddesses invoked by them.

Meir; Middle Kingdom, mid-12th Dynasty (*c*.1900–1850 BC)

National Museums Scotland

Coffin of Tairtsekher

New Kingdom,
early 19th Dynasty (*c.*1300–1250 BC)

National Museums Scotland

NEW KINGDOM

TAIRTSEKHER

DAUGHTER OF IRTNEFRET

EARLY 19TH DYNASTY (c.1300–1250 BC)

There is a coffin in the collections of National Museums Scotland that is typical of the New Kingdom period. It illustrates a short-lived but colourful trend – dating to the reigns of Horemheb (c.1320– 1291 BC) and Rameses II (c.1279–1212) – for decorating coffins in the manner of a living person dressed in their fine linen clothes. The coffin belongs to a young girl, Tairtsekher.

Although the coffin is child-sized, Tairtsekher is shown as an adult wearing a white dress, the fine pleating of which is marked out in red. Her skin is reddish and her braided hair or wig is black. On the trough her hair-braids are picked out with horizontal yellow stripes. On each arm there is a delicate bracelet and wristlet, and she is wearing a pair of gold earrings, and a polychrome or many-coloured collar. The feet have been sculpted in relief with sandals painted on in white.

Tairtsekher's left arm lies across her chest, while the right hangs by her side.

The sides of the trough have been painted with alternate vertical stripes of red and yellow, which become horizontal stripes of black and yellow at the head.

The foot of the coffin (opposite) shows a black standing figure of Isis, lady of Chemmis (the protector of Horus) on the lid, and a *djed*-pillar (indicating the resurrection of Osiris) on the trough. The Isis scene is flanked by a pair of texts, and another runs on the top of the lid between the feet. The texts simply name the young girl, along with her mother, Irtnefret.

The coffin of Tairtsekher might have been one of several coffins from a family group buried in the tomb of the craftsman Sennedjem at the village of Deir el-Medina, Western Thebes. Sennedjem was part of a group of workmen involved in the building of the tombs of the pharaohs in the Valley of the Kings, and who are known to have resided at Deir el-Medina. These workers were a varied group of highly-skilled stonemasons, artists and carpenters who used their skills in their spare time to construct and decorate fine tombs and funerary equipment for themselves, families and friends.

**Outer coffin of Amenhotepiin
(lid and trough) and head of coffin (detail)**

The above detail from the outer coffin shows a sun-disc in the centre flanked by two *uraei* (cobras).

Thebes; Third Intermediate Period,
late 25th Dynasty (*c.*700 BC)

National Museums Scotland

20

THIRD INTERMEDIATE PERIOD
AMENHOTEPIIN
SON OF KHAAMUN AND BAKRI

LATE 25TH DYNASTY (c.700 BC)

As you enter the exhibition space, the magnificent coffin of Amenhotepiin, son of Khaamun and Bakri, catches the eye.

The outer coffin of Amenhotepiin, along with the inner coffin, was one of a group of thirty coffin-sets allegedly found during an excavation carried out in February to March 1869 on behalf of HRH Albert Edward, Prince of Wales, and the Princess of Wales. It came from a tomb at Deir el-Medina in Thebes. However, it is now evident that the coffins had been gathered together for the benefit of the royal party, and probably at no point lay in the specified excavation.

Nineteen of the coffin-sets were presented to the Prince and examined on arrival in Britain by Samuel Birch (1813–1885) at Clarence House in London. The Prince donated the sets to various institutions around the British Isles, including the Pitt Rivers Museum in Oxford, the Fitzwilliam Museum in Cambridge, and the Museum of Science and Art in Edinburgh, now National Museums Scotland.

The wooden and plastered outer coffin of Amenhotepiin has a deep trough and broad, rather flat, lid. The red face has been given a stubby black beard and a wig striped in yellow, green and red (the dominant colours of the coffin), with yellow as the main background colour. There is a fillet or band around the brows, and the top of the head of the lid is adorned with a sun-disc with two *uraei* or cobras.

Below the collar, the chest bears a winged sun-disc. Below this are images of gods such as Thoth leading the deceased from a balance, under which sits another god, Ammit, a crocodile-lion-hippopotamus monster. In front of them are a vertical-bearded serpent, and the gods Re-Harakhty, Osiris, Isis, Nephthys, and the Four Sons of Horus.

The mummy, lying on a lion-bed, with a *ba* or soul flying above, is flanked on each side by a column of text, a *wedjat-eye* and a solar falcon.

The upper surface of the feet is occupied by a recumbent falcon and a *wedjat*-eye, flanked by columns of text which extend onto the sides of the feet.

Coffin of Calisiris

The wooden vaulted coffin of Calisiris was found by Scottish archaeologist Alexander Rhind in 1857. One end of the lid bears five lines of an inscription identifying Calisiris (see detail opposite).

Sheikh Abd el-Qurna, Thebes;
Roman Period (*c.*20 BC)

National Museums Scotland

ROMAN PERIOD
CALISIRIS
OVERSEER OF THE ARMY, SON OF PETOSIRBUCHIS AND TASHERKHONSU

(c.20 BC)

Egypt became part of the Roman Empire in 30 BC, after the defeat of Cleopatra VII and Mark Antony.

During the last years of the Ptolemaic Period, there was a move away from earlier styles in the design of coffins, and the rectangular coffin and wooden sarcophagus returned to favour. The coffin here is typical of the early Roman Period. It was owned by General Calisiris, Overseer of the Army, and the son of Petosirbuchis and Tasherkhonsu. Calisiris had begun his career under Cleopatra before transferring his allegiance to the Romans.

The burial of Calisiris was part of a family group discovered in 1857 by the Scottish archaeologist Alexander Henry Rhind at Sheikh Abd el-Qurna, Western Thebes.

This same burial contained the mummy of his son-in-law, a cavalry officer named Montsaf, who died in 9 BC, and other family members.

The tomb also included the mummy of an unknown woman, now in the collections of National Museums Scotland, who also features in this exhibition. Her story, and that of Alexander Rhind and his discovery at Sheikh Abd el-Qurna, can be found on pages 38–39 and 50–53.

Life and Death in

ANCIENT EGYPT

The practice of mummification in Egypt evolved over several thousand years. The earliest mummification occurred naturally, when bodies were buried in the arid desert sands. Later, the Egyptians began to preserve the bodies of their dead artificially, using an increasingly sophisticated embalming process now known as mummification.

In the beginning mummification was reserved for pharaohs and high-ranking individuals, but gradually it became more common practice. The complexity of the embalming process depended on the status and wealth of the family.

Once the body was embalmed it was laid to rest in a tomb. Several different tomb types developed over the dynasties. These depended upon the status of the deceased and the environment the tombs were set in.

Amulets and jewellery might be placed strategically on the wrapped body to adorn and to protect it. Such amulets were believed to possess magical powers.

Mummy-cases of cartonnage, a type of papier-mâché made of linen or papyrus, and plaster, started to appear in c.900 BC. Cartonnage masks or covers were produced in funerary workshops (see pp. 30–31).

" O my heart ... do not stand up as witness against me ... "

THE BOOK OF THE DEAD

THE ART OF MUMMIFICATION

Step 1: WASHING THE BODY

When the deceased arrives at the embalming house the body is washed with oil and rinsed with water. The brain was sometimes removed through the nose with a hooked probe which was used to break up the putrefying organ, the matter draining out of the nostrils.

Above, left: Canopic chest of Amenhotep

A richly-decorated painted wooden chest containing the four canopic jars where the organs of the deceased, Amenhotep, were placed after removal.

Thebes; Third Intermediate Period, 25th Dynasty (c.700 BC)

Right: Heart amulet

A heart amulet, made from stone and glass, carved with a figure of a man worshipping a seated Osiris, dated c.1500–400 BC

Both images: Rijksmuseum van Oudheden (Leiden, The Netherlands)

Step 2: REMOVAL OF THE ORGANS

The lungs, stomach, intestines and liver were then removed (usually through an incision in the left side of the belly), washed, dried, and preserved in canopic jars (or in later periods wrapped and later returned to the body). As the heart was believed to be the seat of memory and emotion, it had to face judgement before the deceased could move on to the afterlife. It was, therefore, left inside the body, or a heart scarab or vase-shaped heart amulet added as a substitute, if required.

During the Final Judgement, the heart of the deceased was weighed against an ostrich feather symbolising Ma'at, the goddess of truth and justice. If it balanced with the feather, the deceased had lived according to the law of Ma'at and could move on to the afterlife. If the weight of the heart was out of balance, the deceased had lived a life of sin and their heart would be eaten by Ammit, the devourer.

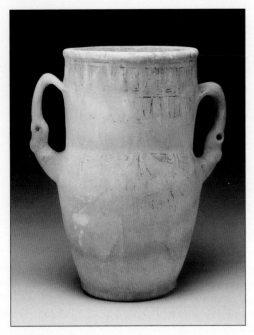

Below: Heart scarab of Seb

In ancient Egypt, the scarab beetle was the incarnation of the sun-god Re in his morning form, known as Khepri, as whom he was reborn every morning. It was believed that the dead shared in this daily resurrection of the sun, so the scarab beetle was a potent symbol of resurrection.

New Kingdom, 18th Dynasty (c.1475 BC)

Rijksmuseum van Oudheden
(Leiden, The Netherlands)

Step 3:
DEHYDRATION OF THE BODY

The body was then covered in natron, a natural salt, and left for around a month. This dehydrated the corpse and eliminated fat. It also acted as an anti-bacterial agent. After a set time, the natron was removed. The body was now rinsed and oils and unguents applied to preserve some skin elasticity. More oil was applied before the body was wrapped.

Above: Unguent vase

This alabaster vase in the shape of an amphora has two handles with gazelle heads. It once carried the name of the reigning pharaoh, Thutmose III.

New Kingdom (1550–1070 BC)

Rijksmuseum van Oudheden
(Leiden, The Netherlands)

Step 4:
WRAPPING OF THE BODY

Wrapping the body was a ritual overseen by an embalming priest, who recited appropriate spells and prayers during the process. He might also place amulets on the mummy or between the bandages to protect the dead on their journey into the afterlife. These amulets were made to represent gods or animals, or perhaps parts of the body.

Wrapping techniques varied with time, but from c.2000 BC onwards, limbs were wrapped individually before further layers of bandages bound the limbs to the body, creating the classic mummy shape. The mummy was then wrapped in a shroud. As the bandages were applied, the wrappings might be coated with liquid resin. This ensured that they remained in place, contoured to the shape of the body.

THE BOOK OF THE DEAD
AND OTHER PAPYRI

At the time of the Middle Kingdom, spells were written on the insides of coffins. Funerary 'books', however, created from rolls of papyrus, were first made in the New Kingdom, around 1550 BC. These 'books' of spells were at first found near the mummy in the burial chamber, or inside a small statue. Later they might be found on the mummy itself.

Spells were included to guide the deceased into the next world, and as a guarantee of successful passage to the afterlife. Ancient Egyptians believed that what was written or depicted could come about magically in the next world.

The most common of such books was the Book of Coming Forth by Day, better known as the Book of the Dead. Other books also existed, including the Book of What is in the Underworld (in Egyptian, *Amduat*), the Book of Caverns, the Book of Gates and the Book of Breathing.

No two papyrus copies of the Book of the Dead were absolutely identical. Each contained a slightly different selection of spells, some were illustrated, others only plain text. Texts might be written in hieroglyphs, but most were in the handwritten form of the script called hieratic, or later in a further handwritten form known as demotic.

Mythological papyrus

This papyrus contains texts and illustrations from different mythological sources. At the top are scenes and texts from the Book of the Dead. Below is a depiction of the sky-goddess Nut arched over her husband, the earth-god Geb. Between them is the air-god Shu, flanked by a pair of *bas*. This latter image is from a source other than the Book of the Dead.

Third Intermediate Period (1070–663 BC)

Rijksmuseum van Oudheden
(Leiden, The Netherlands)

THE CHEST OF LIFE

The containers used for the mummy were often referred to as 'chests of life', and they played a key role in ensuring the eternal life of the deceased.

Depending upon wealth and status, as well as fashion, the mummy could be enclosed in nests of up to three coffins. Until the Second Intermediate Period (*c*.1650 BC), coffins were usually rectangular, but from this point onwards they took the shape of a wrapped and masked mummy. This was referred to as a 'mummiform' or 'anthropoid' style of coffin.

The coffin (sometimes coffins) could be enclosed in a rectangular sarcophagus which was sometimes made of stone. Coffins, however, were usually made of wood and sometimes cartonnage, although for some kings it might even be gold and silver.

Coffins and sarcophagi were usually decorated with texts and images. The purpose of this was two-fold: to provide magical protection and to conjure up the food and drink needed to sustain the deceased for eternity.

AMENHOTEP

PRIEST OF THE GOD AMUN AND AMUN'S WIFE, MUT

THIRD INTERMEDIATE PERIOD, 21ST DYNASTY (c.1000 BC)

This magnificently decorated coffin (see opposite and left) belongs to Amenhotep, a Theban priest of the god Amun and Amun's wife, Mut.

Amenhotep's coffin ensemble is typical of the 19th, 20th, 21st and early 22nd Dynasties (c.1300–900 BC). At this time a mummy-board was placed inside the coffin on top of the mummy. This replaced the mask that had, in earlier times, been placed over the head and shoulders of the deceased.

Scenes and texts relating to the next world were painted on the coffin and mummy-board, including the resurrection of Osiris, the solar cycle of the day and night, Weighing of the Heart, a *ba* bird, a large floral necklace with two falcon heads, Nut (goddess of the sky) with outstretched protective wings, the boat in which the sun travels through the sky, and the goddess Hathor holding an *ankh*, the symbol of life.

Opposite: Coffin and mummy-board (above) of Amenhotep

Thebes; Third Intermediate Period, 21st Dynasty (c.1000 BC)

Rijksmuseum van Oudheden (Leiden, The Netherlands)

CARTONNAGE

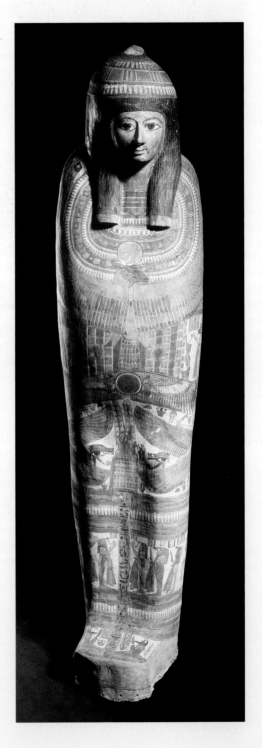

Cartonnage was frequently used for cases, masks or panels, designed to cover all or part of the mummified and wrapped body. Although a cheaper material, and thus more affordable to a greater number of people, it could be gilded and decorated for wealthier citizens.

To create a cartonnage full-body case, a mummy-shaped form was made from mud and straw built around a light reed structure. Up to twenty layers of plaster-soaked linen were applied to the structure. Once dried, an opening at the back of the form was used to extract the mud, straw and reeds.

While the cartonnage was still pliable, the wrapped mummy was pushed into the cartonnage form from below. The back was then laced up with thin bindings and sealed with plaster. A piece of wood was used, like a peg, to close up the opening at the feet.

After a thin coat of white plaster was applied and left to dry, the cartonnage mummy was ready to be

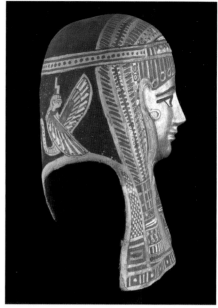

decorated with divine images and texts.

Funerary masks made out of cartonnage started to appear around 2100 BC and lasted until the Roman Period.

Masks provided protection for the mummy's head, but also ensured that the mummy would be recognised by the *ba*, or spirit of the deceased, when it returned to the body. The features of the deceased are idealised, showing how he or she would wish to look in the afterlife.

Funerary masks

Since it was thought that the skin of gods was made of gold, it was appropriate for the faces and hands of masks and coffins to be covered with gold foil. Some masks, like the famous mask of Tutankhamun, were made of solid gold. If gold paint was not affordable, yellow paint was used.

Mask (left):
Ptolemaic Period (304–30 BC)
Rijksmuseum van Oudheden
(Leiden, The Netherlands)

Mask (right):
El-Rubayyat, Fayyum; mid-Ptolemaic period
(3rd or 2nd century BC)
National Museums Scotland

Opposite: Cartonnage of Nehemsu

This cartonnage, for a female mummy, is adorned with inscriptions of her name and title, and an offering formula to the gods Osiris and Re-Harakhty. It is believed that white was used to echo the colour of the wrappings.

Thebes; Third Intermediate Period,
22nd Dynasty (900–800 BC)
Rijksmuseum van Oudheden
(Leiden, The Netherlands)

DECORATION

Depending on the time and social status of the deceased, amulets and jewellery were placed on the wrapped body for adornment and protection. From the 22nd Dynasty (945–730 BC) onwards, a net of blue faience beads, a symbol of the sky, was placed on the mummy. Amulets depicting the four sons of Horus also provided magical protection.

A winged scarab might be placed on the chest. The scarab was the incarnation of Khepri, the Egyptian name for the morning sun, the one who was reborn and a symbol of resurrection. Accordingly, it was

Necklace

Made from gold, glass, carnelian, faience, red jaspis and lapis lazuli.

New Kingdom (c.1539–1075 BC)
Rijksmuseum van Oudheden (Leiden, The Netherlands)

an appropriate amulet to ensure the resurrection of the dead person.

The outermost shroud was typically a plain sheet of linen. During some periods it was dyed red or decorated with images or texts.

Garlands of flowers were sometimes placed on the body. Such simple tributes were common to all levels of society.

THE HOUSE OF ETERNITY

After the body was mummified, decorated and placed in the coffin, it was ready to be taken into the tomb, the 'House of Eternity'. It would now lie for all time, typically facing west towards the setting of the sun.

The tomb might have a chapel above ground, where family, priests and visitors could commemorate the dead and leave offerings. The chapel might have a false door, a *stela* or a statue of the deceased to mark the boundary between the worlds of dead and the living. It was through this that the *ba* and *ka* could move freely between the two worlds.

Funeral of Nebamunn and Ipuky

As depicted in their tomb chapel at Thebes.

New Kingdom, 18th Dynasty (*c*.1370 BC)
© The Trustees of the British Museum /
Copy by Nina de Garis Davies

During the funerary rituals, the 'Opening the Mouth' ritual was performed. The priest would make the breath of life return to the dead, enabling them to speak and eat in the afterlife, magically receiving the offerings left in the chapel.

The body was then taken down to an underground burial chamber, which was sealed after the funeral ceremony. The chamber contained all the objects that the deceased would need in the next world.

33

MUMMIFIED ANIMALS

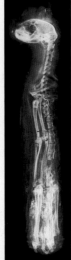

Mummy of a cat (left) and crocodile (above) with x-rays

Cats (*Felix catus*) were associated with the goddess Bastet who had the head of a cat, and many cat mummies were brought as offerings to her temples. Crocodiles (*Crocodilus niloticus*) were also mummified and have been found in necropolises around Egypt. The crocodile was sacred to the god Sobek, depicted with the head of a crocodile.

Graeco-Roman Period (1st–2nd century AD)

Rijksmuseum van Oudheden (Leiden, The Netherlands)

Animals were often mummified in ancient Egypt, but for what purpose?

As some animals were believed to be the earthly incarnations of certain gods, their bodies might be mummi-fied and buried with due ceremony. Cats, ibises, crocodiles, falcons, even baboons, were often mummified, usually for religious purposes.

During the Late and Ptolemaic Periods, mummification of animals became a boom industry. Millions of animals were deliberately raised in order to be mummified and sold to pilgrims as offerings to the gods. A pilgrim to a temple of the cat-goddess Bastet, for example, would take a mummified cat as an offering.

Indeed, so great was the demand for animal mummies that mummy bundles thought to contain an ibis or crocodile, for example, might be found only to contain sand or mere fragments of the bird or animal.

The processes of x-ray or CT scanning can determine the true contents of an animal mummy with-out having to unwrap it.

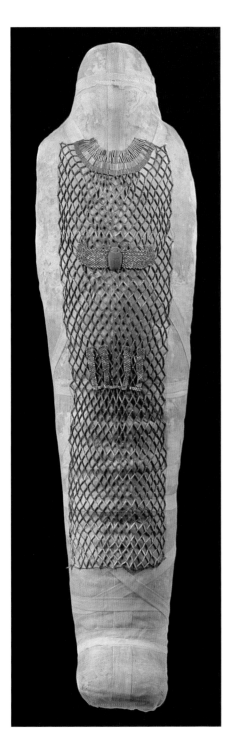

PAWIAMEN

SON OF DJEDHORIUFANKH AND NESIKHONSUPAKHERED

THIRD INTERMEDIATE/ LATE PERIOD, 25TH–26TH DYNASTIES (700–650 BC)

The inscription on his sarcophagus indicates that the mummy featured here is of an adult male named Pawiamen.

Pawiamen was Skipper of the Domain of Amun, meaning that he was in charge of the boat fleet attached to the temple at Karnak. The mummy was purchased in 1828 from the first collection to come onto the market from the diplomat and merchant Giovanni d'Anastasy and it finally arrived at the National Museums of Antiquities in 1829.

A necklace with four strings of beads, a winged scarab, and the four sons of Horus who all have the same head, were placed on the fabric.

Mummy of Pawiamen

Thebes; Third Intermediate/Late Period, 25th–26th Dynasties (700–650 BC)

Rijksmuseum van Oudheden (Leiden, The Netherlands)

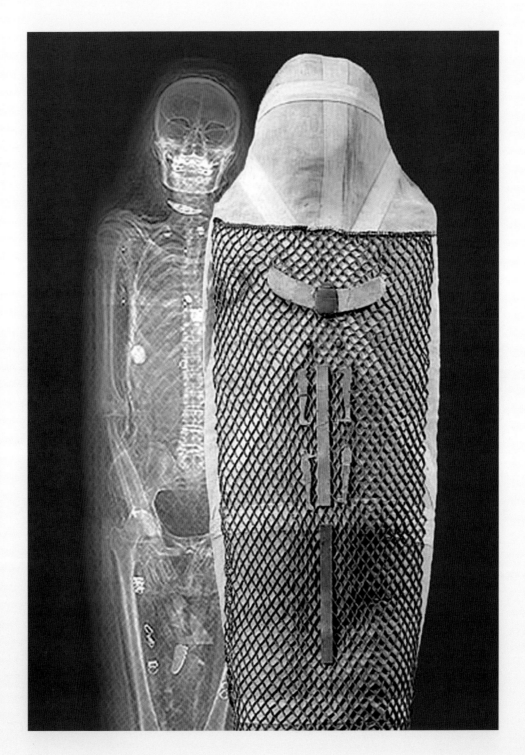

Mummies

WITNESSES TO THE PAST

In modern times, technologies that were often developed for the field of medicine have enabled experts to study mummies using non-invasive techniques. The information we can now gather has expanded our knowledge of this ancient and fascinating civilisation.

Such methods make it possible to learn more about mummification processes and, in some cases, to identify the cause of death. Computerised tomography (CT) scanning can provide quite incredible and enlightening views of the inside of a mummy, making it possible to see the amulets placed between the bandages. It can also lead to the creation of 3D facial reconstructions and even the 3D printing of exact reproductions of different elements, such as the printed copies of hidden amulets included in the exhibition.

The results of various tests and procedures provides researchers with information on the illnesses and diseases suffered by ancient Egyptians, as well as their eating habits and living conditions. It can even offer us an insight into family relationships and the movements of the population.

Opposite: Mummy and CT scan of the priest Ankhhor (pp. 42–47)

Scan results can provide invaluable data concerning anatomy, age and the process of mummification.

Rijksmuseum van Oudheden
(Leiden, The Netherlands)

The Rhind Mummy

Discovered by Rhind in 1857 in the tomb of Montsaf. Amulets on the wrapping during the process of mummification have been identified as follows:

- **[1]** winged scarab
- **[2]** *djed*-pillar
- **[3]** *wedjat*-eyes x 4
- **[4]** crouching, crowned raptor
- **[5]** winged scarab
- **[6]** a pectoral
- **[7]** papyrus sceptre
- **[8]** a pectoral
- **[9]** Four Sons of Horus
- **[10]** lotus flower

National Museums Scotland

Below are some of the results from the 2011 scans, based on CT data obtained at the CRIC (University of Edinburgh).

Source: E. Kranioti/CRIC (University of Edinburgh) in collaboration with National Museums Scotland

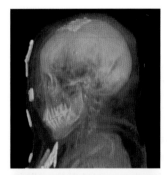

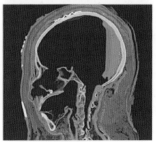

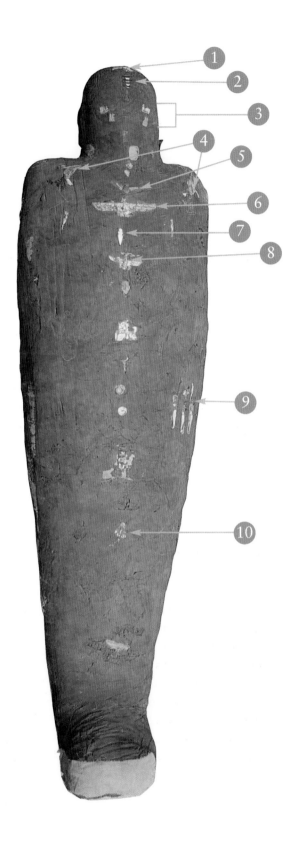

THE RHIND MUMMY
IDENTITY UNKNOWN

ROMAN PERIOD
(c.9 BC)

The story of the Scottish Egyptologist Alexander Henry Rhind and his exciting excavations in 1857 is outlined on pp. 50–53. The mummy (opposite) was found during Rhind's dig and brought back to Edinburgh intact. But what can modern technology tell us?

In Rhind's account he refers to the mummy as having a black, bitumenised cloth surface. However, recent scientific analysis has revealed this bitumen layer to be a composition of beeswax and plant resin.

In 1996 the mummy was examined using a medical CT scanner in Edinburgh as part of the NMS Mummy Project. The scan revealed the embalmed remains of a well preserved adult female. Among the decorative amulets originally placed within the wrappings, there was also evidence of an object on top of the skull and on the right thigh. Identification of these objects at that time, however, was not possible.

In 2011 the scans were repeated using a high resolution scanner at the new Clinical Research Imaging Centre of the University of Edinburgh. Results now revealed that the woman was slightly built and 1.58 metres in height. Her teeth were moderately worn, and she may have suffered toothache from periodontal disease and impacted molars.

During the embalming process several valuable amulets had been included in the wrapping. The scanning process revealed that, in addition to the gilded winged scarab visible on her forehead, there is also a similar scarab of gold foil which had been placed on the top of her head, now beneath the wrappings. A circular gold disc was detected over her midriff, and a rolled scroll is lying under her right hand, against her right thigh.

Detailed measurements of the skeleton made from the CT data confirmed her sex and narrowed her age to 25 to 29 years. They also indicated that the woman was Egyptian in origin, during a period when many individuals in Egypt were of Greek descent.

Cause of death, however, has not been established. Her skeleton shows she was in good health before she died.

SENSAOS-TASHERYTDJEDHOR

DAUGHTER OF SOTER
AND KLEOPATRA-KANDAKE

ROMAN PERIOD (AD 109)

In another tomb dated to the Roman Period (this time to the later emperors Trajan and Hadrian), a mummy of a young girl was buried. Sensaos-Tasherytdjedhor, the daughter of Soter and Kandake, died in AD 109 at the tender age of sixteen years, two months and nine days.

The mummy of Sensaos came into the collections of the National Museum of Antiquities in 1829. The source was the diplomat and merchant Giovanni d'Anastasy (see p. 35), who had purchased the mummy from local plunderers at Thebes. They had found it in 1820, in a tomb at Thebes that originally belonged to a noble of the New Kingdom, named Thutmose. Coffins and mummies from the tomb found their way into various museums around Europe, and were among the first such Roman Period Egyptian items to reach the continent.

The inscriptions on the coffins allow us to identify or understand her lineage. Her mother Kandake, for instance, had a name that was familiar among queens of Nubia (now southern Egypt and

northern Sudan). This pointed to the possibility that Sensaos may have come from this area. Recent reconstructions of her features have also suggested this origin for the young Sensaos.

Sensaos's name appears on her coffin in both the Greek form as 'Sensaos' and in its Egyptian form as 'Tasherytdjedhor'. Alexander the Great had conquered Egypt in 332 BC, and by the lifetime of Sensaos, Egypt was a bi-lingual country with Greek the language of the ruling class.

At her death, according to the custom of the period, Sensaos's mummy was covered with a splendid shroud. But does the face painted on the shroud really belong to her?

In 1998 a CT scan enabled experts to reconstruct Sensaos's face. These digital images provided the raw data to produce a 3D model of her skull using the multi-jet modelling technique. Based on set standards, small wooden pegs were placed on the skull to obtain the correct thickness of the facial tissue and to make it possible to apply muscles and skin in clay.

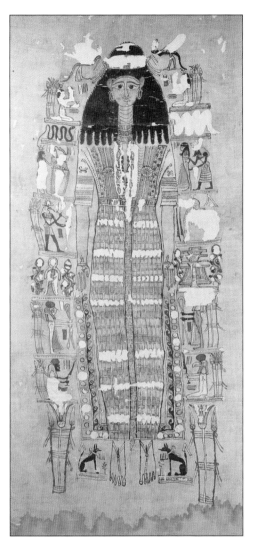

Once the skull was moulded in wax, some skin colouring, artificial eyes and earrings could be added. Her hair would then be styled in the fashion of the period.

Scans also showed that she was about 1.45 metres tall, and that glass eyes had been placed on her eyelids. Her head was turned towards her chest. During the embalming process, the brain had been removed through the nose and an incision made in the abdomen to remove the organs.

When it became possible to compare the face and the shroud, it became apparent that there was no real resemblance. Nonetheless, the very process of reconstruction greatly added to the information already gathered about the girl known as Sensaos.

Decorated shroud (above) and linen wrappings (left) of Sensaos

Thebes; Roman Period (AD 109)

Rijksmuseum van Oudheden
(Leiden, The Netherlands)

Ankhhor on display

The sarcophagus, inner and middle coffins, and the mummy of Ankhhor.

Late Period, c.650–625 BC

Rijksmuseum van Oudheden (Leiden, The Netherlands)

" To speak a dead man's name is to make him live … "

THE BOOK OF THE DEAD

ANKHHOR
PRIEST OF THEBES

The highlight of the *Fascinating Mummies* exhibition is undoubtedly the spectacular mummy of Ankhhor from the National Museum of Antiquities.

From his coffins and sarcophagus we know his name and his profession to be 'Ankhhor, Priest of Montu-Lord-of-Thebes'. Now, through the work of Egyptologists, coupled with modern technology, we are able to discover more about his life, his family and the process of his death.

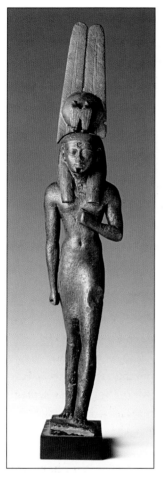

Bronze votive statuette of Nefertem/Montu

This statuette, originally of Nefertem, was later transformed into a representation of the god Montu. The headdress consists of a sun-disc, with two cobras flanked by ostrich feathers, and is associated with the falcon-headed god.

Late Period (712–331 BC)

Rijksmuseum van Oudheden
(Leiden, The Netherlands)

The Book of the Dead of Horemkheb (detail)

This sheet of papyrus is from the Book of the Dead and shows the priest Horemkheb (on the right of the image).

New Kingdom, 20th Dynasty
(1196–1070 BC)

Rijksmuseum van Oudheden
(Leiden, The Netherlands)

ANKHHOR

PRIEST OF MONTU-LORD-OF-THEBES, SON OF HOR AND NESMUT

LATE PERIOD (c.650–625 BC)

Ankhhor was the son of Hor, who was, like his son, another Priest of Montu-Lord-of-Thebes. Hor was married to Nesmut, a Singer of Amun-Re-Lord-of-the-Thrones-of-the-Two-Lands, and they worked in adjoining temple complexes in Luxor or in Thebes.

Montu-Lord-of-Thebes was an Egyptian god, one of whose main temples was situated at Karnak, on the east bank of the Nile at Thebes. He was a patron of war and of the land of the area around Thebes.

However, many members of the priesthood of Montu were buried at Deir el-Bahri, which is on the *west* bank at Thebes. They were discovered under the floors of the temple of Queen Hatshepsut, which dates back eight centuries before Ankhhor was born. It is therefore thought that Ankhhor may have been buried originally in this temple as well.

As one of the priests in the god Montu's great temple, Ankhhor would have carried out daily ceremonies and assisted in the regular festivals.

In Egyptian tradition, the pharaoh was the only personal link between mankind and the gods who protected the cosmos, of which Egypt was the centre. Rituals were thus devised that were intended to keep the god fed and happy, and thus well disposed towards mankind. The upkeep of such rituals and responsibilities could, however, be delegated from the pharaoh to the priests, the 'servants of the gods', who would perform the daily rituals on his behalf. A statue of the god was kept in the sanctuary, ready to be inhabited by his or her spirit when it visited the temple.

The larger temples would have been managed by the high priest and his deputies, assisted by the more junior priests. Ankhhor himself was a middle-ranking member of Montu's priesthood and would have been involved in the temple's administration.

Like the other priests, his education would have been that of a scribe, using a simplified version of hieroglyphic script (hieratic), written on either papyrus or ostraca (fragments of pottery and limestone).

At his death, Ankhhor was mummified and granted a funeral according to his social status. In keeping with the custom of the time, his wrapped body was placed in a pair of mummy-shaped coffins before being enclosed in a rectangular wooden sarcophagus.

The design of Ankhhor's coffins indicates a date of manufacture around 650–625 BC, during the reign of King Psamtik I. This date was established by comparing the coffins and sarcophagus to those of other individuals, whose dates have already been established. This is usually possible by deciphering the information on coffins, where links to particular rulers are evident.

The decoration of Ankhhor's coffin also has protective images and speeches of various divine beings, as well as magic formulae intended to generate food and drink in the next world.

The mummy itself is adorned with a bead net, incorporating a winged scarab and representations of the Four Sons of Horus, flanking two strips of gilded cartonnage.

It is thought that the burial of Ankhhor and his family may have been discovered first by Giovanni Battista Belzoni, the famous Italian excavator and explorer. He is known to have once owned the coffin of Ankhhor's sister, Taawa (now in the Rosicrucian Museum, San José, California), and is also recorded as having undertaken excavation work at Deir el-Bahri. However, as the old records are incomplete, it is possible that local robbers found the tomb of Ankhhor and his family and sold the coffins to Belzoni.

An early 19th-century traveller, Colonel B. E. A. Rottiers, then acquired Ankhhor's mummy, coffins and sarcophagus in Greece or Turkey. How they got there is not known, although their origin in Thebes is not in doubt.

The coffin ensemble of Ankhhor was finally bought in 1826 by the National Museum of Antiquities. However, due

Right: Sarcophagus of Ankhhor

Late Period, c.650–625 BC

Rijksmuseum van Oudheden (Leiden, The Netherlands)

Opposite: Mummy and scan of Ankhhor

Rijksmuseum van Oudheden (Leiden, The Netherlands)

to an earlier decision of the museum's first director, Caspar Reuvens (1793–1835), to forbid the unwrapping and dissecting of mummies, Ankhhor's mummy has remained intact.

What was initially discovered about Ankhhor came from the study of the hieroglyphs on his coffins and the adornments placed on his mummy. Then, in 1965, x-rays provided the first glimpse inside the wrappings.

CT scanning was used to examine the body in 1999. The results were analysed by Egyptologist Maarten J. Raven and radiologist Wybren K. Taconis, providing useful insights into Ankhhor's anatomy, his age and the process of his mummification.

The scans showed the shape and location of amulets and objects placed by embalmers between the wrappings and on the body during mummification. These included a plate, decorated with an Eye of Horus and a scarab, placed over the abdominal incision where the organs were removed to ensure that evil spirits could not enter the body.

Ankhhor was approximately 1.60 metres tall, and he died between the ages of 32 and 50 years old. His teeth were in good condition, which was uncommon in ancient Egypt.

Mummification, it appeared, had been properly carried out. The organs and brain were removed, but his heart left inside. It was not possible, however, to determine the cause of Ankhhor's death.

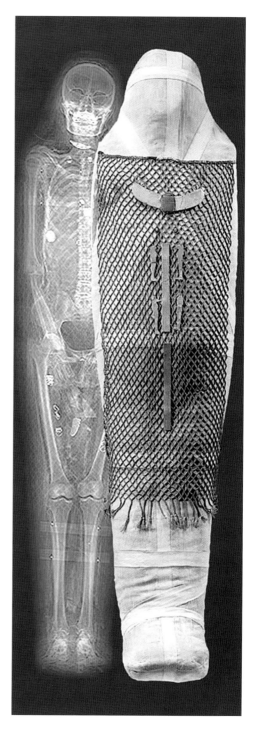

Coffin of Estate-Overseer Khnumhotep, son of Nebtu

An early surviving example of a human-shaped coffin painted white, with four yellow bands with black edging encircling the lid and base. The lid shows a man with a black-painted wig, gilded face, black-painted eyebrows and inlaid-stone eyes. A false beard is attached to the chin, with gold foil to indicate texture and a black-painted strap at the sides of the face.

Deir Rifeh; Middle Kingdom,
second half of 12th Dynasty (c.1800 BC)

National Museums Scotland

The Ancient Egypt Collection in

NATIONAL MUSEUMS SCOTLAND

National Museums Scotland today is the largest multi-disciplinary museum in Scotland. It has around four million items in its collections, including artefacts from the natural world, world cultures, art and design, and science and technology.

The museum has a remarkable, yet little known, Ancient Egypt collection built up from three main sources – the University of Edinburgh, the Society of Antiquaries of Scotland and the Royal Scottish Museum. From its nineteenth-century beginnings, the collection has grown to include spectacular coffins, mummies and artefacts. The vivid iconography and hieroglyphic texts provide a fascinating insight into ancient lives.

In 1996 the NMS Mummy Project was launched, designed to apply a range of scientific techniques to reveal information about the collections. This included a systematic programme of CT scanning of the mummies, facial reconstructions and the examination of grave goods. Much of the knowledge gained about the mummies has come from this continuing project.

The *Ancient Egypt* gallery at the recently reopened National Museum of Scotland can be found on Level 3. Displays include the coffin of an estate-overseer known as Khnumhotep, a royal burial group from Qurna in Western Thebes, and a double-coffin of two young boys called Petamun and Penhorpabik.

In the *Discoveries* gallery, next to the *Grand* gallery, you will find a coffin trough and mummy of Iufenamun, a high-ranking priest, and the coffin lid of the important priestess Tjentweretheqau. These form a display dedicated to Scottish engineer Colin Scott-Moncrieff (pp. 54–55). And in the exhibition itself, the coffin of an army officer Calisiris (pp. 22–23, 53), and the anonymous mummy of Alexander Henry Rhind's 1857 excavations, are also on display (pp. 38–39, 53).

Right:
Portrait of Alexander Henry Rhind
(1833–1863)

Source: Society of Antiquaries of Scotland

Below:
Sheikh Abd el-Qurna

The house where Rhind was based while undertaking his excavation work at Thebes. This is how it would have looked during his time there. The house was built by Henry Salt (1780–1827), a British Consul in Egypt who sponsored a number of early excavations.

Image from Rhind, *Thebes: Its Tombs and their Tenants Ancient and Present* (1862)

National Museums Scotland

YESTERDAY AND TODAY: SCOTTISH ARCHAEOLOGY

A number of distinguished Scots have added greatly to the understanding of ancient Egypt and its history. Such individuals include Joseph Stratton (1778–1840), Alexander Henry Rhind (1833–1863), Colin Scott-Moncrieff (1836–1916), William Matthew Flinders Petrie (1853–1942), Edwin Ward (1880–1934) and Cyril Aldred (1914–1991).

Caithness-born Rhind became interested in archaeology in his teens. In 1853, while studying law in Edinburgh, he was laid low with lung disease. To escape the damp chill of the Scottish climate, he spent time in England, France and Egypt.

Rhind undertook excavations in Egypt mainly around Luxor (ancient Thebes). He was one of the first excavators to record his discoveries in detail for future publication. His collection of Egyptian artefacts included many now in the collections of National Museums Scotland.

Rhind's promising career was cut short when he died in July 1863, aged 29. He was in Italy, on his way home from Egypt. Rhind is buried in Wick parish churchyard.

" Much of the material Rhind … left to the nation is of first-rate importance … "

CYRIL ALDRED, 1955

In 1857, two tombs were discovered by Alexander Rhind at Sheikh Abd el-Qurna at Western Thebes.

Rhind was working with a gang of men when they came across a large tomb with a six-columned hall and lower burial chamber. Sadly, all that remained within the tomb were smashed coffins, tattered strips of linen, and mummies which had been 'ripped up along the throat and breast'.

Rhind found 14 mummy-labels among this mess. They had been used to tag the mummies of princesses of the 18th Dynasty, including daughters of Thutmose IV (*c.*1400–1390 BC) and a royal granddaughter. The labels had been created and placed in the tomb during the reign of Pasebkhanut I (*c.*1014 BC). This had been done at a time when ancient bodies were being moved to protect them from robbery. In this case, the bodies had been brought from the nearby Valley of the Queens.

Then, just ten metres to the south of the princesses' place of burial, a

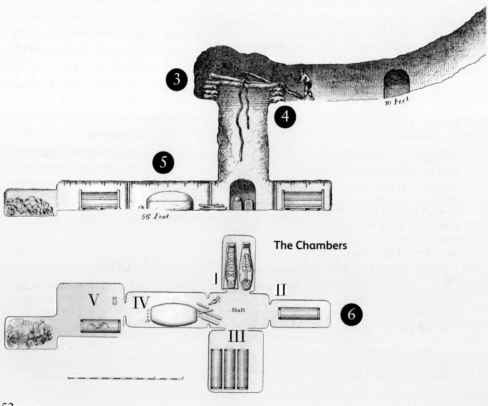

56 feet

The Chambers

52

doorway to another tomb was discovered. This was also a re-used structure, originally constructed during the 14th/13th centuries BC, but re-occupied in early Roman times.

In this complex tomb of passages and chambers (see diagram below), Rhind discovered a family group who had lived soon after Egypt had become part of the Roman Empire in 30 BC.

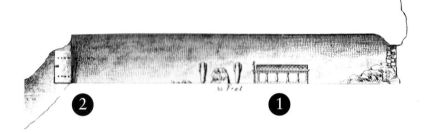

THE TOMB OF MONTSAF

In the entrance passage to the tomb there was a canopy **[1]** which was inscribed for a cavalry officer named Montsaf. He died in 9 BC during the time of the Emperor Augustus. Montsaf was the son of Menkara and his wife Tesherpimont.

The end of the passage marked the end of what had been the chapel of the tomb when it was originally built. Here a wooden door **[2]** led into a corridor going down to the burial chambers. These were accessed from a vertical shaft **[3]**, over which an ancient lifting frame was found **[4]**.

At the foot of the shaft there were a number of low-roofed chambers **[5]**.

The layout of the chambers is illustrated in the bottom section of Rhind's illustration **[6]**.

Chamber I

Two coffins were found in this chamber. Both contained adult mummies, plus the mummies of two children.

Chamber II

Behind a closed wooden door, Rhind and the excavators found the coffin and mummy of Calisiris, Overseer of the Army. He was the son of Petosirbuchis and Tasherkhonsu.

Chamber III

Three rectangular coffins were discovered here, including that of Tabia, wife of Montsaf and the daughter of Calisiris.

Also in chambers III/V there was an unknown adult female buried in one of the coffins. This female, known as the 'Rhind Mummy', is described on pp. 38–39.

Chamber IV

The granite sarcophagus, which was taken over by Montsaf from the tomb's original owner, was contained in this chamber. There were also the mummies of a dog, an ibis and a snake, and the figure of a hawk.

Chamber V

A rectangular wooden sarcophagus was found in this chamber.

Images from Rhind (1862), *Thebes: Its Tombs and their Tenants Ancient and Present*

National Museums Scotland

IUFENAMUN

PRIEST OF AMUN-RE AT KARNAK AND CHIEF OF CEMETERY WORKS IN THE ESTATE OF AMUN-RE

THIRD INTERMEDIATE PERIOD, EARLY 22ND DYNASTY (MID- TO LATE 10TH CENTURY BC)

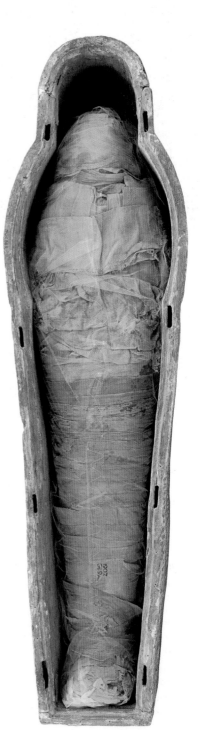

The *Discoveries* gallery in the National Museum of Scotland highlights some of the greatest scientists, writers and thinkers to have studied or worked in Scotland.

Among their number is Edinburgh-born Colonel Sir Colin Scott-Moncrieff (1836–1916), a distinguished Scottish engineer and Under-Secretary of State for Public Works in the Egyptian Government between 1885 and 1891.

From his time in Egypt, Scott-Moncrieff donated a coffin lid, mummy and coffin trough to his former school, Edinburgh Academy. It was transferred to the then Royal Scottish Museum in 1907 and is now an important part of the collections of National Museums Scotland.

The mummy was recorded as being that 'of a man: outer vestment partially destroyed, but having its spirally wound bandages intact'.

It was received with the coffin trough and the mummy has lain in the trough ever since. The coffin lid, however, does not belong to the mummy, but to an important priestess of Amun known as Tjentweretheqau (also called Tamut), possibly the grandmother of the mummy in the coffin.

The texts on the coffin show the mummy to be that of Iufenamun, a high-ranking priest in the temple at Karnak, who is historically well known.

Although the location of the tomb of Iufenamun was certainly Thebes, nothing is known about the exact whereabouts of the entire coffin. The decoration of coffin points to a date of early 22nd Dynasty, during the second half of the 10th century BC.

Above:
Coffin lid of Tjentweretheqau (Tamut)

Egypt, early 21st Dynasty
(late 11th or early 10th century BC)

National Museums Scotland

Opposite: Coffin trough of Iufenamun

Colonel Sir Colin Scott-Moncrieff (right), a Scottish engineer, brought the coffin trough of the high-ranking priest Iufenamun back from Egypt in the late nineteenth century, along with the coffin lid of Iufenamun's grandmother, Tjentweretheqau (above).

Egypt, early 22nd Dynasty,
(mid- to late 10th century BC)

Image of Colonel Scott-Moncrieff from Hollings, *The Life of Sir Colin C. Scott-Moncrieff* (1917)

National Museums Scotland

At least some of Iufenamun's titles are listed on his coffin-trough; it is possible that others were given on his lost coffin lid. They read:

> *The Osiris, Senior Pure-Priest,*
> *Entering-Priest for the Memorials*
> *of Amun-in-Ipetsut, Chief of the*
> *Cemetery for Works in the Estate of*
> *Amun-Re, King of the Gods,*
> *Iufenamun.*

These indicate that Iufenamun ('He who belongs to Amun') was a senior priest of Amun-Re, as well as having responsibility for work carried out in the Theban cemeteries. It is likely that he was the man of the name mentioned on the coffins of Sety I and Rameses II as being, with his father Nesypaqashuty, responsible for moving the mummies of these pharaohs from their plundered tombs in the Valley of the Kings to a safer location (*c.*960 BC), and also one of the men tasked with the burial of the High Priest of Amun, Panedjem II, in a tomb at Deir el-Bahri.

The results of the CT scanning confirmed Iufenamun's status, revealing a high quality of embalming which, with evidence of individually wrapped limbs

and packing beneath the skin, was typical of its time. Four packages of embalming material were also detected, perhaps containing the internal organs, which had been deposited within the cavity of the thorax.

Recent scanning of the body, using non-invasive techniques has further revealed that the man was a mature adult, probably near forty years of age. There are no obvious signs of trauma or indications of the cause of death.

The high quality coffin trough has been made from sycamore-fig wood that has been plastered and painted, and a resin varnish added. It was then decorated in a yellow coffin style typical of the period, with a colour scheme based on red ink on a yellow ground, over-painted in red, green and blue-green pigment, with a yellow varnish.

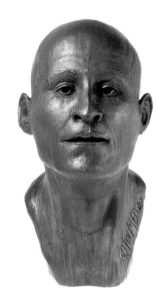

The face of Iufenamun

Using a plaster model of Iufenamun's skull created from CT scans, a medical artist was able to build up the facial muscles and skin in clay, before casting the completed face of Iufenamun in bronze.

National Museums Scotland

Below and opposite (details): Coffin trough of Iufenamun

The left or 'east' side of the coffin trough is decorated with images of Iufenamun with Egyptian gods, including Isis and Osiris, Nut (goddess of the skies), Hathor (the cow goddess) and Amun-Re, the creator deity. These images represent the afterlife and rebirth, and were intended to offer protection to the deceased.

The details on the coffin trough (opposite, top to bottom) show goddess Nephthys on the head-end of the trough; gods and goddesses on a boat, with Ammit (left) and a snake-headed goddess; and a *djed*-pillar on the foot-end of the trough.

Egypt; early 22nd Dynasty, (mid- to late 10th century BC)

National Museums Scotland

THE 'QURNA QUEEN' AND CHILD
IDENTITIES UNKNOWN

17TH DYNASTY
(16TH CENTURY BC)

In 1908 the eminent Egyptologist Sir William Matthew Flinders Petrie (1853–1942) discovered the intact burial of a woman and child at Qurna, Western Thebes, on the road to the Valley of the Kings. With its gold jewellery, ceramics, food offerings and furniture, it was at that time, according to Flinders, 'the richest and most detailed undisturbed burial that has been completely recorded and published'.

Petrie offered the group to the Royal Scottish Museum, now National Museums Scotland, on the promise that the whole tomb group would remain together. It included 'a coffin of the Aahmen style, ten pots in beautifully-made string mats, most of which have more or less preserved

---

Coffin of the 'Qurna Queen'

On this coffin the *rishi* patterning is gilded and painted in blue with black details on a yellow ground. The face is framed by a striped linen *nemes*-cloth, a beaded collar with falcon terminals, and a vulture-pectoral with outstretched wings.

Qurna, Western Thebes; 17th Dynasty (16th century BC)
National Museums Scotland

with collodian. A blue marble dish with four apes. A horn with ivory bird-head spout. An obsidian and an alabaster khol pot of fine work. Two bead net pouches with handles. A head rest with inlaid stem of ivory and ebony. Two baskets, and sundry.'

The 'Qurna' burial has intrigued scholars and researchers since it was first discovered. First of all, the burial had been excavated in an area where other royal burials had already been found. Second, the coffin and grave goods, including gold jewellery, were of such high quality and richly decorated. All of this pointed to the possibility of a royal burial.

Unfortunately, the area where her name and titles had once been inscribed had been damaged – possibly when the child's coffin was placed upon it – and only the traces of the first hieroglyph survive today, suggesting the first sign of one of the titles of a royal wife. But her exact identity, and that of the child, remain a mystery.

What can be confirmed, however, is that the woman's coffin is typical of 17th Dynasty decorative style at Thebes. It is anthropoid in shape and contains the body without having a separate outer coffin. It also has a particularly Theban feather design around the body of the coffin, showing the deceased as a human-headed bird (the *ba* or released soul). This type of design is known as *rishi*, after an Arabic word for 'feathered'.

Coffin of the 'Qurna child'

Questions remain concerning the identity of the child buried in this coffin, and what the relationship is between the child and the woman found in the coffin at Qurna.

Qurna, Western Thebes;
17th Dynasty (16th century BC)
National Museums Scotland

A group of ceramics from the burial is of a type known as Kerma ware – pottery vessels made in Nubia. Nubia was also a known source of gold and a region that was, at this point, an independent state. Could the mummy of Qurna have been a Nubian princess?

The Qurna burial and grave goods have been extensively studied through the Mummy Project at National Museums Scotland, set up to look at this and other questions. When the coffins were originally opened and the

mummies unwrapped, they were found to be poorly mummified and today only the bones remain. It is now known that the adult mummy is that of a young woman, probably in her late teens or early twenties, about 1.56 metres tall and left-handed. There were no obvious signs pointing to a cause of death.

Petrie himself suggested that the woman's skull was not typically Egyptian. However, a thorough examination of her skeleton to determine whether she was Nubian or Egyptian was inconclusive.

The coffin itself is constructed out of wood, with tamarisk for the lid and sycamore-fig for the case. It was covered in a fine plaster or gesso, painted and then gilded. Pigments used included Egyptian blue, calcite, carbon and

Buried treasure

The grave at Qurna contained objects which indicated a high level of wealth. The woman's mummy wore a magnificent collar of gold rings, a pair of gold earrings, two pairs of gold bracelets, and a girdle of fine electrum rings.

National Museums Scotland

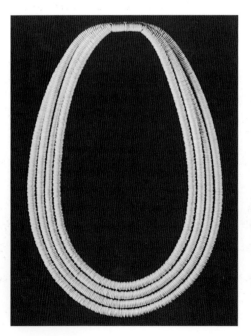

orpiment, a yellow colour obtained from arsenic tri-sulphide.

The child was estimated to be between two and three years old, but again no cause of death was found and it is not possible to determine directly from the remains whether the child is a boy or a girl.

The relatively simple white-painted rectangular coffin without inscriptions is not an indication of status or identity in this case. It is also not possible to conclude whether the child was a relative, perhaps a sibling or offspring, of the young woman.

The two coffins and the grave goods can be seen in the National Museums of Scotland's *Ancient Egypt* gallery, on Level 3, adjacent to the *Fascinating Mummies* exhibition.

Above:
The reconstructed face of the 'Qurna Queen'
National Museums Scotland

Below:
The coffin and grave goods at Qurna
Image from Petrie, *Qurneh* (1909)
National Museums Scotland

Glossary

akh – an 'effective spirit' that could influence affairs in the land of the living

Amduat – funeral text, meaning what is in the Underworld, known as *Duat*

Ammit – 'the Devourer', a crocodile-lion-hippopotamus monster that ate up the parts of the accursed dead in the Judgement Hall of the god Osiris

amulet – charm, often used for protection

Amun(-Re) – chief god of Thebes

ankh – symbol of enduring life

anthropoid – human-shaped

Anubis – god of embalming, represented with the head of a jackal

Aten – religious cult of the sole-god Aten, founded by Akhenaten and Nefertiti

ba – the soul, the eternal force of a human, often depicted as a bird in tombs

Book of the Dead – known also as the Book of Coming Forth by Day; collection of magical writings placed in tombs since the New Kingdom to assist deceased in the afterlife; other 'books' include the Book of What is in the Underworld (in Egyptian, *Amduat*), the Book of Caverns, the Book of Gates and the Book of Breathing

canopic jars – term 'canopic' is derived from the jars with human heads honouring Osiris discovered at Canopus near Alexandria

cartonnage – term used by Egyptologists for the material made from linen/papyrus, glue and plaster used for coffins and masks

CT scanning – computerised tomography scanning

djed-pillar – hieroglyph linked to the myth of the god Osiris

Duamutef – mortuary genius and Son of Horus

dynasty – from Greek; a line of hereditary rulers

faience – from French, after an Italian town, Faenza; a glazed ceramic, usually blue or green

fillet – a band

Final Judgement/Judgement of the Dead – decision by the gods on the afterlife of the deceased

Geb – Earth god, husband of Nut

gesso – fine plaster mixture

Great and Small Enneads – group of nine gods or deities

Hapy – god of the Nile; one of the Four Sons of Horus

Hathor – goddess of sky, love, mirth, beauty and fertility, represented in either human or cow form

hieratic script – a simple form of hieroglyphics

hieroglyphics – from Greek *hierogluphicos*, meaning sacred writing; the ancient Egyptian form of writing using pictures (*hieroglyphs*)

Horus – god of the Sun; son of Isis and Osiris

Hyksos – an Asiatic people who founded a kingdom in Northern Egypt during the 15th and 16th Dynasties

Imseti – a god

Isis – goddess of fertility and nature; sister-wife of Osiris, mother of Horus

ka – life force; the immortal part of a being; often portrayed by a symbolic door painted or carved on the wall of a tomb

Karnak – the northern part of Luxor and the site of many temples

Khepri – Egyptian name for the morning sun

Luxor – city occupying the east bank at ancient Thebes

Ma'at – goddess of truth and justice, cosmic order

mummy – term derived from 7th-century Arabian word for corpses, *mummiya*, meaning bitumen or black resin

naos – from Greek, *naos*, temple, sanctuary with divine statues

National Museums Scotland, Edinburgh – formerly the Industrial Museum of Scotland (1855–64); Museum of Science and Art (1864–1904); Royal Scottish Museum (1904–85); now National Museums Scotland (1985–)

natron – natural salt found in the Wadi Natrun, between Alexandria and Cairo

Neith – one of the four tutelary goddesses of the dead, a goddess of warfare and hunting

nemes-cloth – striped cloth headdress

Nephthys – sister of the gods Osiris, Isis and Seth

Nut – goddess of the sky; wife of Geb

orpiment – yellow colour derived from arsenic tri-sulphide

Osiris – god of the dead and resurrection; brother-husband of Isis; murdered by brother Seth; the first mummy

ostraca – from Greek, *ostrakon*; fragments of pottery and limestone used for writing or sketching

pectoral – piece of jewellery which covers the upper chest

pharaoh – from Greek/Hebrew *par'oh*, or 'Great House'

polychrome – many-coloured

priests – 'servants of the gods' who performed daily rituals, often in temples, dedicated to Egyptian gods

Qebehsenuef – one of the Four Sons of Horus

Re-Harakhty – the sun god

rishi – Theban decoration of coffins, using a feather design, from Arabic word for 'feathered'; pattern found on coffins and masks of 17th and early 18th Dynasties

sarcophagus – stone or wooden outer container; often decorated with images and hieroglyphics, designed to protect the body and its inner coffin

scarab – beetle, a symbol of resurrection as the incarnation of the sun god Re in his morning form, known as Khepri

Seth – god of chaos, brother and murderer of Osiris

shabti – magical servant figure found in tombs from the mid-Middle Kingdom onwards

Sobek – a god, shown with the head of a crocodile

stela – from Greek; monumental stone slab with carvings

Thebes – New Kingdom capital of Egypt, now Luxor

Thoth – ibis-headed secretary of the gods, god of wisdom and the moon

uraeus – a cobra

Valley of the Kings – desert valley at Western Thebes, where the kings of the New Kingdom were buried

Valley of the Queens – desert valley at Western Thebes, where some of the queens, princes and princesses of the New Kingdom were buried

wedjat-eye – the eye of Horus

Image Credits and Acknowledgements

© Rijksmuseum van Oudheden (Leiden, The Netherlands) pages 1, 28 and 29 (Amenhotep, coffin and mummy-board AMM 2-a, 2-b); 8 (stela of Sehetepibreankh AP 21); 9 (*Ba* bird L.IX.30); 25 (Amenhotep, canopic chest AH 183-e) (heart amulet EG-ZM 2710); 26 (unguent vase AAL 10a) (heart scarab of Seb L.II.1); 27 (Mythological papyrus AMS 34 sh. 3); 30 (Nehemsu, cartonnage AMM 2-c); 31 (funerary mask EG-ZM18); 32 (necklace AO 3d); 34 (cat mummy AMM 16b and crocodile mummy AMM 16k, and x-rays); 35 (Pawiamen, mummy AMM 6-a); 36 (Ankhhor, mummy RO.III-e and CT scan); 41 (Sensaos, shroud AMM 8-b); 42–43 (Ankhhor, coffins and mummy RO.III-a, b, c and e); 44 (votive statuette of Nefertem/Montu H.III.M…-2) (papyrus from Book of the Dead AMS 33 sh. 1); 46 (Ankhhor, sarcophagus RO.III-a); 47 (as page 36); and with thanks to the staff of the Rijksmuseum van Oudheden who have assisted in the production of this publication.

© National Museums Scotland pages 11–13 (Montsaf, funerary papyrus A.1956.313); 14 (jar A.1911.210.15) (bowl A.1899.265.7) (beads A.1910.111 5D); 15 (sledge A.1964.461) (cramp A.1977.228 B); 16–17 (Khnumhotep, coffin A.1979.203); 18 (Tairtsekher, coffin A.1887.597 A); 20 (Amenhotepiin, coffin A.1869.33 A); 22–23 (Calisiris, coffin A.1956.351+A); 31 (funerary mask A.1901.547.1); 38 (mummy A.1956.352 and scans); 48

(Khnumhotep, coffin A.1907.713.5); 54 (Iufenamun, trough A.1907.569 A); 55 (Tjentweretheqau, coffin lid A.1907.569 B); 56–57 (details of Iufenamun, trough A.1907.569 A); 57 (Iufenamun, reconstruction V.2010.40.1); 58 (Qurna coffins A.1909.527.1A and 10A); 60 (necklace A.1909.527.19); 61 ('Qurna Queen', reconstruction, NMS); and with thanks to the staff of NMS who have assisted in the production of this publication.

© Aidan Dodson for page 6 (map); and with thanks for his kind assistance with the production of this publication.

© Society of Antiquaries of Scotland for page 50 (portrait of Alexander Henry Rhind). We are grateful to the Society of Antiquaries of Scotland for permission to reproduce this image.

© The Trustees of the British Museum for page 33 ('Funeral of Nebamunn and Ipuky' from John H. Taylor, *Death and the Afterlife* [Chicago: University of Chicago Press]; copy by Nina de Garis Davies)

M. A. Hollings (1917): *The Life of Sir Colin C. Scott-Moncrieff* (London: James Murray), for page 55.

A. H. Rhind (1862): *Thebes: its Tombs and their Tenants Ancient and Present* (London: Longman, Green, Longman & Roberts), for pages 50 and 52–53.

W. M. F. Petrie (1909): *Qurneh* (London: British School of Archaeology in Egypt) for page 60–61.

Bibliography

ALDRED, C. (1955): *Dynastic Egypt in the Royal Scottish Museum* (Edinburgh: HMSO).

BUCKLEY, S. A. (2001): 'Organic chemistry of embalming agents in Pharaonic and Graeco-Roman mummies', *Nature*, vol. 413.

D'AURIA, S. et al. (1988): *Mummies & Magic: The Funerary Arts of Ancient Egypt* (Boston: Museum of Fine Arts).

DAWSON, W. R. (1927): 'On Two Egyptian Mummies preserved in the Museums of Edinburgh', *Proceedings of the Society of Antiquaries of Scotland* (1926–27).

DODSON, A. M. (2009): 'Alexander Henry Rhind at Sheikh Abd El Gurna', *Kmt. A Modern Journal of Ancient Egypt* 19/4.

DODSON, A. M. and S. IKRAM (2008): *The Tomb in Ancient Egypt: Royal and Private Sepulchres from the Early Dynastic Period to the Romans* (London: Thames & Hudson).

DODSON, A. M. and J. J. JANSSEN (1989): 'A Theban Tomb and Its Tenants', *Journal of Egyptian Archaeology* 75.

EREMIN, K. A., E. GORING, W. P. MANLEY and C. CARTWRIGHT (2000): 'A Seventeenth Dynasty Egyptian Queen in Edinburgh', *Kmt. A Modern Journal of Ancient Egypt* 11/3.

EREMIN, K., W. P. MANLEY, A. SHORTLAND and C. WILKINSON (2002): 'The Facial Reconstruction of an Ancient Egyptian Queen', *Journal of Audiovisual Media in Medicine* 25/4.

HOLLINGS, M. A. (1917): *The Life of Sir Colin C. Scott-Moncrieff* (London: James Murray).

IKRAM, S. ed. (2005): *Divine Creatures: Animal Mummies in Ancient Egypt* (Cairo: American University in Cairo Press).

IKRAM, S. and A. DODSON (1998): *The Mummy in Ancient Egypt: Equipping the Dead for Eternity* (Cairo: American University in Cairo Press).

MacLEOD, R. I., A. R. WRIGHT, J. McDONALD and K. EREMIN (2000): 'Historical Review, Mummy 1911-210-1', *Journal of the Royal College of Surgeons of Edinburgh*, 45/1.

MANLEY, W. P. (2006): 'The Identity of an Important Priest in the Collections of the National Museums of Scotland', in Solkin ed. (2006), pp. 71–76.

MANLEY, B. and A. DODSON (2010): *Life Everlasting: National Museums Scotland Collection of Ancient Egyptian Coffins* (Edinburgh: NMS Enterprises Limited – Publishing).

MILLAR, W. F. (1892): 'Notice of an Egyptian Funeral Canopy and of Other Objects in the National Museum bearing Hieroglyphic Inscriptions', *Proceedings of the Society of Antiquaries of Scotland* 26.

MINIACI, G. (2011): *Rishi Coffins and the funerary culture of Second Intermediate Period Egypt* (London: Golden House Publications).

MURRAY, M. A. (1900): *Catalogue of Egyptian Antiquities in the National Museum of Antiquities, Edinburgh* (Edinburgh: Society of Antiquaries of Scotland).

— (1903): *Guide to the Collection of Egyptian Antiquities* (Edinburgh: HMSO).

PETRIE, W. M. F. (1909): *Qurneh* (London: British School of Archaeology in Egypt).

— (1931/32): *Seventy Years in Archaeology* (London: Low, Marston & Co.).

RAVEN, M. J. and W. K. TACONIS (2005): *Egyptian Mummies: Radiological Atlas of the Collections of the National Museum of Antiquities in Leiden* (Turnhout: Brepols).

RHIND, A. H. (1862): *Thebes: its Tombs and their Tenants Ancient and Present* (London: Longman, Green, Longman & Roberts).

RIGGS, C. (2005): *The Beautiful Burial in Roman Egypt: Art, Identity, and Funerary Archaeology* (Oxford: OUP).

ROYAL SCOTTISH MUSEUM (1910): *A Guide to the Collections* (Edinburgh: HMSO).

SOLKIN, V. V. ed. (2006): *Ancient Egypt, 2. On the Occasion of the 150th Birthday Anniversary of Vladimir S. Golenischeff* (Moscow and St Petersburg: Maat).

STRUDWICK, N. and J. H. TAYLOR eds (2003): *The Theban Necropolis: Past, Present and Future* (London: British Museum Press).

STUART, J. (1864): *Memoir of the Late Alexander Henry Rhind of Sibster* (Edinburgh: Neill & Co.)

TATE, J. (2011): 'The NMS Mummy Project: A Summary', internal report (Edinburgh: National Museums Scotland).

TATE, J., K. EREMIN, L. TROALEN, M. F. GUERRA, E. GORING and B. MANLEY (2009): 'The 17th Dynasty Gold Necklace from Qurneh, Egypt', *ArchaeoSciences* 33.

TATE, J. and S. KIRK (2011): 'Examination of the Rhind Mummy (A.1956.352)', internal report AR2011/83 (Edinburgh: National Museums Scotland).

TATE, J., S. KIRK, E. KRANIOTI, et al. (forthcoming): 'Examination of the Rhind Mummy (A.1956.352)', report to be published (Edinburgh: National Museums Scotland).

TROALEN, L., M. F. GUERRA, J. TATE and B. MANLEY (2010) 'Amazing Dynasty 17 Jewellery from Qurneh', *Decorated Surfaces on Ancient Egyptian Objects* (J. Dawson, ed.).

WARD, E. (1912): *Guide to the Collection of Egyptian Antiquities* (Edinburgh: HMSO).

WILLEMS, H. (1988): *Chests of Life: A study of the Typology and Conceptual Development of Middle Kingdom Standard Class Coffins* (Leiden: Ex Oriente Lux).